MW00715620

PARABLES OF
Jesus

MELISSA C. DOWNEY AND SUSAN L. LINGO

PAGE DESIGN AND ILLUSTRATION BY ROY GREEN

COVER ILLUSTRATION BY TERRI STEIGER

STANDARD
PUBLISHING
Cincinnati, Ohio

Scripture quotations are from the *International Children's Bible, New Century Version,*
copyright © 1983, 1986, 1988 by Word Publishing, Dallas,Texas 75039. Used by permission.
The *International Children's Bible* must be used to solve the puzzles.

Library of Congress Catalog Card Number 93-85774

ISBN 0-7847-0142-3

Copyright ©1994 by Melissa C. Downey, Susan L. Lingo
Published by The STANDARD PUBLISHING Company, Cincinnati, Ohio.
Division of STANDEX INTERNATIONAL Corporation. Printed in U.S.A.

Parables of Jesus

A parable is a special kind of story. In a parable, one thing that is easily understood is used to explain something else that might be harder to understand. For example, Jesus told parables about coins and rocks and sheep and other things that His listeners knew about. This way, Jesus knew that most people would understand His lessons!

Jesus told parables to teach us important lessons about faith and love and being the way God wants us to be. He used parables because He knows we learn easier by hearing stories than by trying to remember long lists of rules!

Jesus also knows that there is a big difference between hearing and listening! Sometimes, we hear something but we do not understand what has been said because we aren't really listening. This is why Jesus said, "You people who hear me, listen!" (Matthew 13:9) Jesus knew that some people who heard Him had unloving hearts—they heard His words but they did not listen to the meaning. They did not really want to understand because they did not want to change.

Jesus told His parables nearly 2000 years ago! But as old as the parables are, they are still true today. The words of Jesus will still be true tomorrow and for always!

Even though Jesus' parables never change, some of the letters below do need to be changed! Use the code to change the letters to find out what the parables of Jesus do for us.

Change E to S	Change O to U	Change T to A
Change S to E	Change U to O	Change A to T

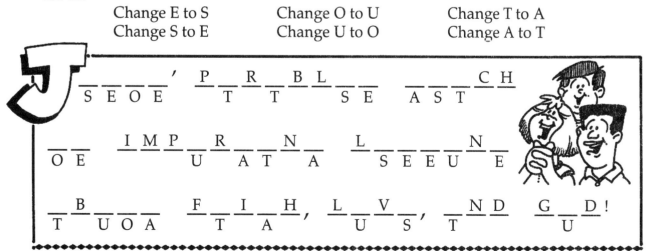

```
___ ___ ___ ___ '  P  _  R  B  L  _  ___ ___ ___  C  H
 S  E  O  E       T     T     S  E   A  S  T

___ ___  I  M  P  _  R  _  N  _  L  ___ ___ ___  N  _
 O  E              U     A     A     S  E  U     E

___  B  ___ ___  F  _  I  _  H  ,  L  _  V  ,  ___  N  D  G  ___  D !
 T   U   O  A      T     A          U     S '  T            U
```

©1994 by Melissa C. Downey and Susan L. Lingo.
Permission is granted to reproduce this page for ministry use only—not for resale.

The Sower and the Seeds

A 🧑‍🌾 went out to plant some seeds. Some of the seeds fell on the hard road and 🐦🐦 ate it all up! Some seeds fell on 🪨. It began to grow but soon died because there was little soil and no water. Some seeds fell in thorny weeds. These seeds grew, but soon the 🌿 choked out the good little plants. Some seeds fell on good ground. These seeds grew and made 100 times more grain seeds!

What does this parable mean?

The seed is like God's Word. The hard road is like people who hear God's Word with a hard heart. They do not give God's Word a chance to grow in their lives. Then Satan (like the birds) steals this seed away.

The rocks are like people who hear God's Word and quickly believe, but they do not send down strong roots of faith. They do not feed and water their budding faith with more of the Lord's Word. Their new faith soon dies.

The thorny ground is like people who hear God's Word and let it grow, but then let other things like worry, or fear, or greed choke out their new faith. Their faith does not grow because they do not put God first in their lives!

The good ground is like people who hear God's Word with love and honesty inside their hearts. They are willing to learn God's Word. They send down strong roots of faith and love, and obey God. God's Word grows and produces good things in their lives! Then, just like the seed that grows in good soil and produces more seed, these people are able to use the good things in their lives to share God's love with others!

What kind of ground are you?

Will your heart be ready to receive the Word of God?
Will you feed and water your new faith with more of God's Word?
Will you grow deep roots of faith?

©1994 by Melissa C. Downey and Susan L. Lingo.
Permission is granted to reproduce this page for ministry use only—not for resale.

Sneak Peek

This simple science project will allow you to watch roots as they grow!

You Need:
    clear glass jar
    potting soil
    paper towels
    bean seeds

Directions:
1. Dampen two paper towels and fold them to fit around the inside of the jar.
2. Fill the jar with potting soil. Be careful to keep it *inside* the paper towels.
3. Stick the bean seeds *between* the glass and the paper towels (so that you can see them from the outside).
4. Set jar in a sunny spot and keep the soil moist.

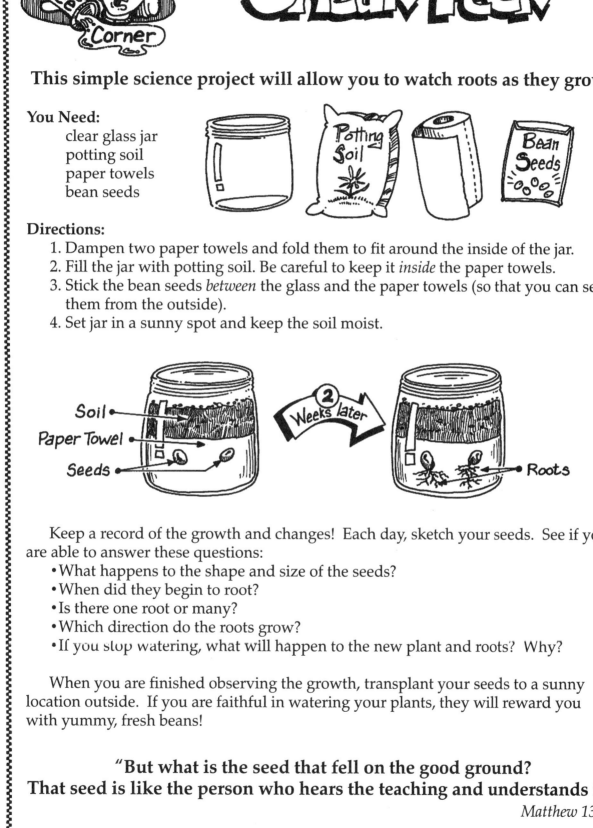

Keep a record of the growth and changes! Each day, sketch your seeds. See if you are able to answer these questions:
- What happens to the shape and size of the seeds?
- When did they begin to root?
- Is there one root or many?
- Which direction do the roots grow?
- If you stop watering, what will happen to the new plant and roots? Why?

When you are finished observing the growth, transplant your seeds to a sunny location outside. If you are faithful in watering your plants, they will reward you with yummy, fresh beans!

"But what is the seed that fell on the good ground?
That seed is like the person who hears the teaching and understands it."
Matthew 13:23

©1994 by Melissa C. Downey and Susan L. Lingo.
Permission is granted to reproduce this page for ministry use only—not for resale.

Ready, Set GROW!

The parable of the sower and the seed was one of the first of the many parables that Jesus told. Why? Well, as we have learned from the parable, before a plant can grow, it must first be planted in good ground. Then it must send down long roots to feed and water itself.

Jesus had many, many things to teach us about God. He knew that God's Word was like a precious seed. He wanted us to be ready to hear and understand God's Word. We need to be like the good ground—ready to receive the seed and able to send down strong roots of faith into our hearts. Jesus told this parable early so we would be ready for His next lessons!

Jesus wants us to get ready, get set, GROW!

What happens when we get ready to hear God's Word? We plant His Word deep inside our hearts! And what happens when God's Words of wisdom and truth are planted in faithful hearts? Use the code below to help you find the answer!

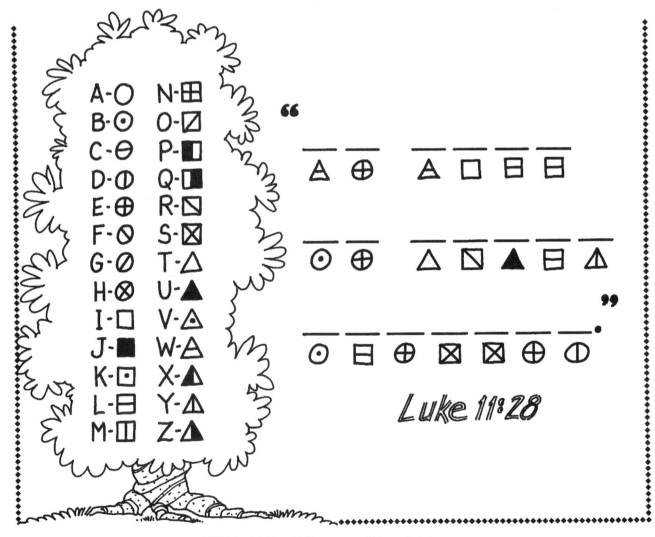

Luke 11:28

©1994 by Melissa C. Downey and Susan L. Lingo.
Permission is granted to reproduce this page for ministry use only—not for resale.

The Reason for Roots

Did you know that without roots, plants would die? Roots allow plants to live because they act like a drinking straw and an anchor. How do they do this? Read on!

Plant roots are like deep, growing straws through which a plant is fed. A plant sends out roots in search of nitrogen for food and oxygen from water. Nitrogen and oxygen are two elements God put in the earth and the air to help all living things grow and live. A plant needs roots to find nitrogen and oxygen. Without long, deep roots to drink up food and water, a plant cannot live!

Roots are also like an anchor for plant. Just as a big anchor keeps a ship from floating away, long, strong roots keep plants on the ground. Roots help a plant stay in place when a strong wind blows!

Jesus teaches us in the parable of the sower and the seed that the Word of God must be deeply rooted inside our faithful hearts. Through our roots of faith, God will feed us with His love and with the food for life found in His Word. When trouble comes along, we will not be blown away if our roots of faith are long and deep. We must grow long, deep roots to keep us anchored in Jesus!

The pictures below are out of order. Color them and cut them out. Now glue them in the correct order (as a seed grows) to see a Scripture about keeping our roots of faith deep in Jesus.

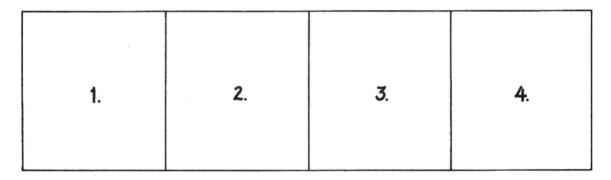

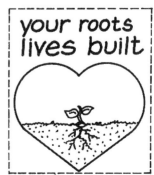

©1994 by Melissa C. Downey and Susan L. Lingo.
Permission is granted to reproduce this page for ministry use only—not for resale.

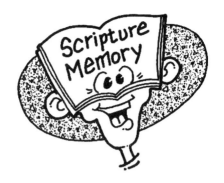

And what is the seed that fell on the good ground? That is like those who hear God's teaching with a good, honest heart. They obey God's teaching and patiently produce good fruit.

Luke 8:15

When we have grown long, deep roots of faith and love from the seed of God's Word, we become like healthy plants! We grow qualities that are like God's qualities. These good, godlike qualities are called "fruits." When good qualities grow and produce more good qualities, God has produced His good fruit in us! Some of God's good fruits are love, kindness, forgiveness, and helping others. Other good fruits are faith, patience, wisdom. God wants us to grow these things in our lives and share them with others!

Put some seeds of God's Word into your heart by making this

Good Fruit Scripture Mobile

Directions:
1. Copy the apple and leaf patterns onto another piece of paper.
2. Color the apple and leaf. Glue them to stiff paper and cut out.
3. Cut the apple apart on the dotted lines.
4. Tape fishing line to the back of each piece of apple. Leave a space between each piece. Leave a long end to use in hanging up your mobile.
5. Glue the leaf to the top of the apple.
6. Hang your mobile from the ceiling or in a doorway.

©1994 by Melissa C. Downey and Susan L. Lingo.
Permission is granted to reproduce this page for ministry use only—not for resale.

The Lost Sheep and Lost Coin

A 🧑‍🦱 had **100** 🐑 but **1** wandered off and got lost. The 🧑‍🦱 left his **99** 🐑 and went to look for the lost 🐑. He did not **STOP** until he found it. The happy 🧑‍🦱 carried his 🐑 home. He called his friends and neighbors to share his joy. He said, "Be 😊 with me because I have found my lost 🐑." (Luke 15:3-6)

A 👧 lost **1** of her **10** silver 🪙. It was very precious to her. She lit her 🪔 to look for the 🪙. She cleaned her 🏠 from top to bottom until she found her 🪙. The happy 👧 called her friends and neighbors. She said, "Be 😊 with me because I have found the 🪙 that I lost." (Luke 15:8,9)

What do these parables mean?

It may seem silly to care so much about one coin when you have nine others. Or to care about one sheep when you have 99 others. But in these two parables, Jesus teaches us that every single one of us is *very* valuable to God! Can people get lost from God? Yes, sometimes people disobey God and turn away from Him. But because God loves each one of us very much, He will not stop searching for people who wander away from Him. And every time one of these lost people comes back to God, Jesus says there is much happiness in Heaven (Luke 15:10)!

God told the prophet Ezekiel exactly how He felt about His lost sheep (people). What God said is recorded in the Bible and is a promise for you and me—today! To find out what God promised, write in the letter of the alphabet that comes *after* the letter shown below the spaces.

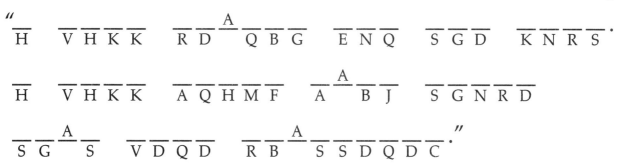

"___ ___ ___ ___ ___   ___ ___   ___ ^A___ ___   ___ ___ ___   ___ ___ ___   ___ ___ ___ ___ .
H V H K K   R D   Q B G   E N Q   S G D   K N R S

___ ___ ___ ___ ___   ___ ___ ___ ___ ___   ___ ^A___   ___ ___   ___ ___ ___ ___ ___
H V H K K   A Q H M F   A B   J   S G N R D

___ ^A___   ___ ___ ___ ___   ___ ___   ___ ^A___ ___ ___ ___ ___ ."
S G S   V D Q D   R B   S S D Q D C

©1994 by Melissa C. Downey and Susan L. Lingo.
Permission is granted to reproduce this page for ministry use only—not for resale.

1 One for All

The shepherd in the parable of the lost sheep left his whole flock to look for one lost lamb! Jesus did not say that the lost lamb was the most beautiful, or had the best wool, or was the shepherd's favorite. It was simply one lost sheep.

Sometimes we forget how very special each one of us is to God, our Shepherd! How wonderful that He *never* forgets! There may be flocks and flocks and flocks of people in God's kingdom, but each one of us is valuable to God BECAUSE . . . .

All Things Come From One

Every potato that grows underground
           11   10

Or each shiny pumpkin all golden and round
   3   14   9

Is nurtured along by the rain and the sun
                           6

But started in time where there was but ONE.
    1   2

Though you may think we all came from two,

That Adam and Eve made me and made you,
        8

We all had our start in the heart of just ONE;
         5   4

Our heavenly Father is where we come from!
 7   13   12

Use the numbered letters from the poem above to fill in the numbered spaces below and you will find one **1-derful** Scripture!

" __ __ __ __ __ __ __ __ __ __ __ __ __ __ __ __
  1 2 3 4 3   5 6   7 8 3   9 7 10   11 8 10

__ __ __ __ __ __ __ __ __ __ __ __ __ __ __ __ __ __ __ ."
12 11 1 2 3 4   7 12   3 13 3 4 14 1 2 5 8 9

(Ephesians 4:6)

©1994 by Melissa C. Downey and Susan L. Lingo.
Permission is granted to reproduce this page for ministry use only—not for resale.

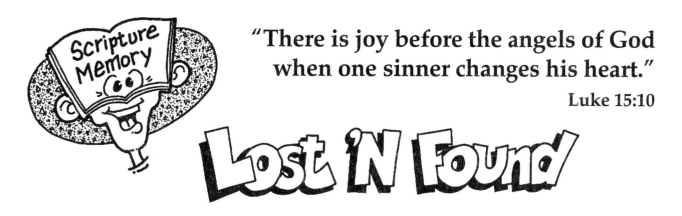

"There is joy before the angels of God when one sinner changes his heart."

Luke 15:10

Lost 'N Found

Have you ever lost something important to you? Then, did you find it? If you have, you know how good it feels to find something that was lost.

People, like toys, clothes, or animals, may become lost. Lost from God. They wander away from His love searching for something that they think will make them happy. Of course, people are much more important than lost things, and God is very sad because of these lost people. That is why God sent Jesus to earth.

"The Son of Man came to find lost people and save them." (Luke 19:10)

Jesus came to find the lost, but he also teaches *us* to be finders! If we love all people, we will help them find their way back to the Good Shepherd. And when we do, something wonderful happens in Heaven!

The memory verse is repeated below, but some words are missing! Color, cut out, and glue the pictures at the bottom of the page in their correct spaces to complete the verse. As you work, try to memorize the verse.

"There is ☐ ☐ ☐ the ☐ of ☐ when ☐ sinner changes his ☐ ."

©1994 by Melissa C. Downey and Susan L. Lingo.
Permission is granted to reproduce this page for ministry use only—not for resale.

The Great Cover Up

In Jesus' parables of the lost sheep and the lost coin, a shepherd and a woman search until they find their precious one. Play the game below to see if you can be the first to find your #1 sheep or coin.

You need:

Game strips below (Color them with bright colors!)
2 dice
18 pieces of paper this size

Object of the game: Be the first player with *only* the #1 uncovered.

Directions (for two players):

1. Cut out the 2 game strips. One player will have the sheep, the other will have the coins.

2. Players take turns rolling 1 die or 2 (the choice is yours). Cover *either* the numbers shown on the dice, *or* the combination of the numbers shown. For example, if you roll a 4 and a 3, you may either cover up your #4 and #3 spaces, or your #7 space (since 4 and 3 add up to 7).

3. If a player rolls a 1 while rolling 1 die, he loses that game because he must cover his #1 space!

4. The first player to have only his #1 space uncovered (all the other spaces are covered) is the winner!

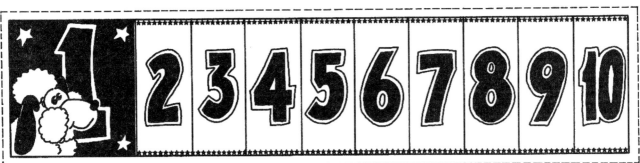

©1994 by Melissa C. Downey and Susan L. Lingo.
Permission is granted to reproduce this page for ministry use only—not for resale.

Lost Words

In the parable of the lost coin, a woman searched for a lost coin. Now it is your turn to search for lost words! Words from the parable in Luke 15:8-10 are hidden in the puzzle below. First, fill in the missing words and then find each one in the puzzle.

"Suppose a _____ has _____

silver _____ , but she _____ one of

them. She will _____ a _____ and

clean the house. She will _____

_____ for the coin until she

_____ it. And when she finds it, she will

call her _____ and neighbors and say,

'Be _____ with me because I have

_____ the coin that I lost!' In the

_____ way, there is _____

before the _____ of _____ when

one _____ changes his _____ ."

```
S T I C E N P L O Y W H F I N D S R A E
R W O M A N R T F R I E N D S I H T P G
T S H P J Q U H O A P A B T A S P E O A
A Y E L O S E S T I J R E C M E R N I A
N D R R Y I F I N S K T F O E M O D N S
L W B E Y N C A R E F U L L Y P L E T L
I E B S L N O G H N O L H A E H A P P Y
G O D E N E I M N O U D N L E N A P O N
H J L E T R N C S A N G E L S B O G Y T
T E L A S W S O V C D N E H L O O K D E
T N A L A M P I F R I K N T M O T S T A
```

©1994 by Melissa C. Downey and Susan L. Lingo.
Permission is granted to reproduce this page for ministry use only—not for resale.

The Talents

Based on Matthew 25:15-30

A rich man was going on a long trip. He gave three of his servants some talents (money) to look after until he came back. To the first servant, he gave five talents, to the next, two talents, and to the last one he gave one talent. The rich man gave to each servant what that servant was best able to handle.

The first two servants wisely invested the money and made twice as much. The third servant buried his money in the ground.

When the owner came back, he asked his servants what they had done. The first two brought him the talents he had given them and the talents they had earned. The owner was very pleased and gave them more. They shared in his happiness. The third servant brought back the only talent the owner had given him.

The owner was angry because the servant had not used the talent wisely. "You lazy servant," he shouted, "you should have invested the money!" Then the owner told the other servants to "Take the money from him and throw him out!"

What does this parable mean?

When God made you, He gave you the ability to do some things well. We call these abilities, "talents." Our talents are gifts from God, just like the money called talents was a gift from the owner. Like the owner, God wants us to use our talents wisely. He does not want us to waste the gifts that He gives to us. Some people have the talent to sing, or paint beautiful pictures, or write wonderful stories. Some people have the ability to listen patiently as others talk about their problems. Some people have the ability to share what they have willingly and happily. All of these abilities and talents are gifts from God.

Don't Bury Your Talents!

When we say, "I can't," we are burying our talents—our gifts from God. God says "You can!" How do we know this?

Color over all the J's and W's to find the answer.

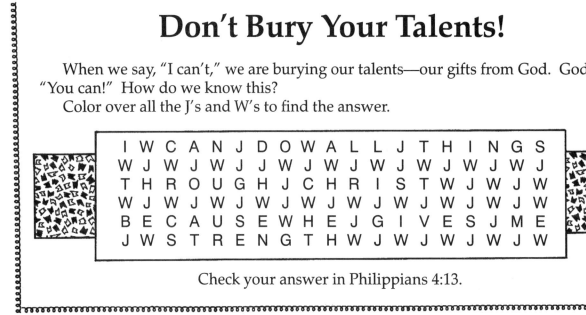

```
I W C A N J D O W A L L J T H I N G S
W J W J W J J W J W J W J W J W J W J
T H R O U G H J C H R I S T W J W J W
W J W J W J W J W J W J W J W J W J W
B E C A U S E W H E J G I V E S J M E
J W S T R E N G T H W J W J W J W J W
```

Check your answer in Philippians 4:13.

©1994 by Melissa C. Downey and Susan L. Lingo.
Permission is granted to reproduce this page for ministry use only—not for resale.

"God has shown you his grace in giving you different gifts. And you are like servants who are responsible for using God's gifts."

1 Peter 4:10

What gifts (talents/abilities) has God given you? Draw pictures of the things you are able to do well on the boxes below. Then cut out the boxes as a puzzle. When you put the pile of presents back together, the Scripture on the back will be correct, too. You may also work the puzzle from the other side, learning the verse as you put the words in the correct order.

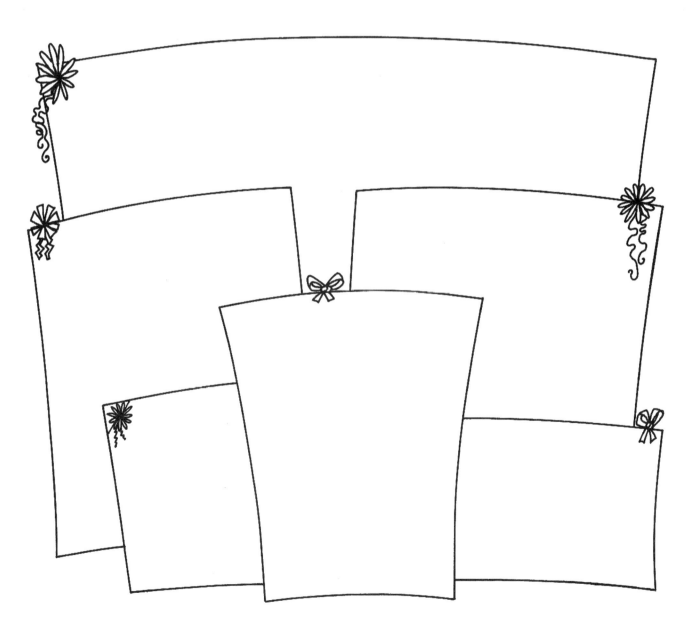

©1994 by Melissa C. Downey and Susan L. Lingo.
Permission is granted to reproduce this page for ministry use only—not for resale.

God has shown you his grace

in giving you different gifts.

And you are like servants

who are responsible

for using God's gifts.

1 Peter 4:10

©1994 by Melissa C. Downey and Susan L. Lingo.
Permission is granted to reproduce this page for ministry use only—not for resale.

Feet Are Neat!

Based on 1 Corinthians 12:12-26

Hand was very sad. He wanted more than anything else in the world to be like Foot. "Feet are neat!" he said to himself. "Feet can jump, run, walk, and skip. Feet can't be beat! Oh, I wish I could do the things that Foot can do!" The longer Hand thought about being like Foot, the sadder he became.

Foot heard what Hand was saying and chuckled to himself, "Oh, Hand doesn't know how hard it is to do the things I do!" Then Foot said to Hand, "Hey, Hand! You've got the story all wrong! Being a foot is tough! I have to bear the weight of the whole body—and that's heavy, man! I usually have to go first through the rain and snow. Sometimes shoes are too tight, and I often get sweaty in socks. It's not *always* neat being feet! Besides, Hand, if you did what I do, how would Man hold his tools or throw a ball or draw a picture? How would he eat an ice cream cone or wave 'Hello'? No, Hand, your jobs are much too important for you to become like me!"

Hand was pleased with what he heard. He hadn't realized just how important he really was!

Just how special are you?

Have you ever felt like Hand? Have you ever wished that you could do the things others can do? God has given each of us special gifts. He wants us to discover our gifts and develop them. He wants us to remember that each of us is unique and important.

Look at your hands, your fingers, your thumb. Do you see the tiny lines? No one has lines just like yours! God made your hand print, your fingerprint, your thumbprint just for you! Did you get that? *No one else in the world has prints exactly like yours!!*

Thumbs Up! Use your *unique* thumbprint to make some thumbprint pictures!

Needed:
  paper
  an ink pad
  fine line markers
  a few willing thumbs

Directions:
  Gently press a thumb on the ink pad and then on a sheet of paper. Several prints may be made from one inking.

  Notice that everyone's prints are unique—special!

  Using fine line markers, make pictures from the prints. Some ideas are shown, see if you can think of others!

©1994 by Melissa C. Downey and Susan L. Lingo.
Permission is granted to reproduce this page for ministry use only—not for resale.

Based on Matthew 7:24-29

A wise built his upon solid rock. day, the gathered in the sky. Rain fell and flood waters came . The wind blew hard against the wise 's , but the did not fall down! The did not fall because it was built on a foundation of solid rock!

Another man was very foolish. He built his on sand. When the came and the floods came , the sand began to shift. The wind blew hard against the foolish 's and it crashed apart! The on the sand fell apart because it was built on a weak foundation!

What does this parable mean?

This is a parable about building our lives on a strong foundation. A foundation is what a building is built on. Let's say you are going to build a house with wooden blocks. If you build your house on a bare floor, the foundation is very firm. If you build your house on thick carpet, the foundation is less steady. If you build your house on a wobbly card table, your house will probably fall down when you bump the table!

With the parable of the wise and foolish builder, Jesus teaches us to choose our foundation carefully. Some people think that being pretty, or popular, or having lots of expensive toys will make them happy. They think that these things will always make them feel important. They build their lives on these sorts of things, putting their faith in prettiness, or popularity, or money. But what happens when trouble comes? Lots of money cannot protect us from evil! Expensive toys do not make us wiser! A handsome face will not attract friends if we are ugly on the inside.

Jesus teaches us that we must build our lives on the truth that comes from God. The Lord must be the most important part of our lives! And if we build our lives on God's Word, we will not fall apart when trouble comes.

©1994 by Melissa C. Downey and Susan L. Lingo.
Permission is granted to reproduce this page for ministry use only—not for resale.

Though storms may blow and floods may flow, a house built on rock will never be shaken! Make a Rock 'N Roll Jar to remind you of "The Rock!"

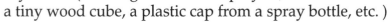

You need:
    baby food jar (with lid)
    hot glue and glue gun
    a rock that will fit inside the jar
    a tiny house (from a game of Monopoly ™,
      a tiny wood cube, a plastic cap from a spray bottle, etc.)

Directions:
1. Glue the rock to the inside, bottom of the jar.
2. Glue the house on top of the rock.
3. Fill the jar half full of water and screw on lid.
4. Cut out the verse below and fold the paper on the dotted lines. Glue the tabs to the lid so that the verse stands upright.

Now, no matter how much you shake, rattle, and roll the waters, your house will stand firm! Use this as a paperweight for your desk to remind you of your solid foundation! (This makes a nifty gift, too!)

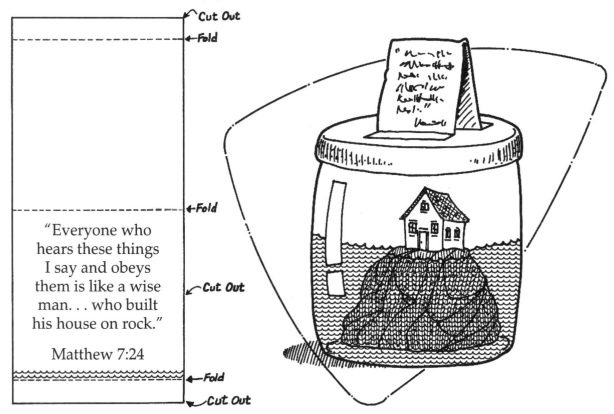

Cut Out
Fold
Fold

"Everyone who hears these things I say and obeys them is like a wise man. . . who built his house on rock."

Matthew 7:24

Cut Out
Fold
Cut Out

©1994 by Melissa C. Downey and Susan L. Lingo.
Permission is granted to reproduce this page for ministry use only—not for resale.

Building a firm Foundation

You're in a store when a shiny display catches your eye: a MOUNTAIN of soup cans stacked as high as can be! You reach out to snatch one from the very bottom—but wait! Do you know what will probably happen if you take away that important can from the bottom foundation? The mountain may CRASH down around you!

A strong foundation supports a building and the most important stone in the foundation is called "the cornerstone." The cornerstone is important for two reasons: it is the first stone placed in a foundation and it serves as a reference point for all the other stones. That means, the builder checks the placement of the cornerstone to see how the foundation is supposed to be built. Do you see the meaning behind the statement that Jesus is our cornerstone? As we build our foundation of faith on the Word of God, we look to Jesus to give us direction.

There are things we can do to strengthen our foundation of faith. To find three good things, write down the letter that comes *before* the letter shown under the space.

1. $\overline{}\,\overline{}\,\overset{A}{\overline{}}\,\overline{}\,\overline{}$ $\overline{}\,\overline{}\,\overline{}\,\overline{}'\overline{}$ $\overline{}\,\overline{}\,\overline{}\,\overline{}$.
   M F A S O   H P E T   X P S E

2. $\overline{}\,\overline{}\,\overset{A}{\overline{}}\,\overline{}\,\overline{}\,\overline{}$ $\overline{}\,\overline{}\,\overline{}$ $\overline{}\,\overline{}\,\overline{}\,\overline{}$.
   Q S A J T F   U I F   M P S E

3. $\overline{}\,\overline{}\,\overline{}\,\overline{}\,\overline{}$ $\overline{}\,\overline{}\,\overline{}\,\overline{}\,\overline{}\,\overline{}$.
   T F S W F   P U I F S T

©1994 by Melissa C. Downey and Susan L. Lingo.
Permission is granted to reproduce this page for ministry use only—not for resale.

You believers are like a building that God owns. That building was built on the foundation of the apostles and prophets. Christ Jesus himself is the most important stone in that building.

Ephesians 2:20

Building a strong foundation is no puzzle! Just let **Jesus** be the **Rock** who holds you firmly! Carefully cut out the stones below and use them to build the foundation underneath the wise man's house. As you work, see if you can memorize the verse.

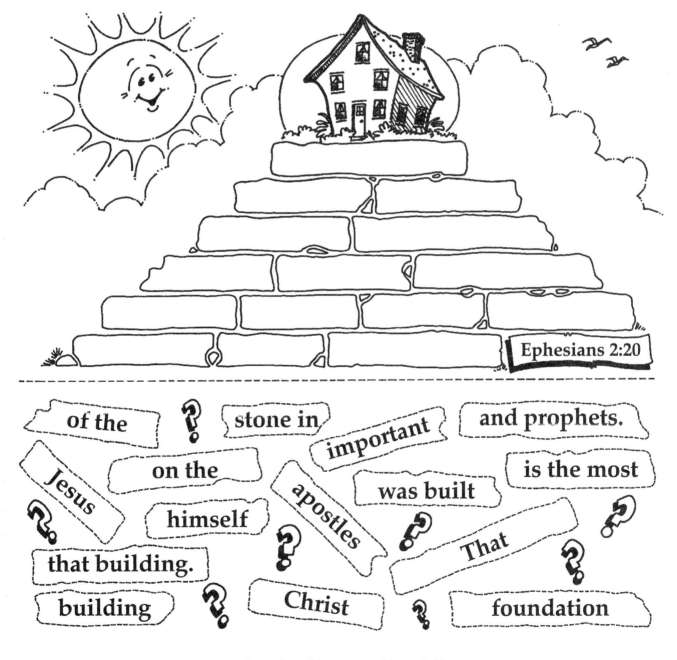

Ephesians 2:20

of the · stone in · important · and prophets. · Jesus · on the · apostles · was built · is the most · himself · That · that building. · building · Christ · foundation

©1994 by Melissa C. Downey and Susan L. Lingo.
Permission is granted to reproduce this page for ministry use only—not for resale.

Based on Luke 10:25-37

Jesus taught that two of God's laws are the most important laws. First, you are to love the Lord your God with all your heart, all your soul, all your strength, and all your mind. Secondly, you are to love your neighbor as much as you love yourself.

One day, a man asked Jesus, "Who is my neighbor?" Jesus told a parable to answer the man's question. Jesus said that the events in His story happened on the road between Jerusalem and Jericho. The people listening to Him knew that this was a very dangerous road. It winds between high, rock walls that are full of places for robbers to hide. What was the story that Jesus told? We call it, "The Good Samaritan."

The Good Samaritan

A man was traveling down the road from Jerusalem to Jericho. A gang of robbers saw him and attacked him. They ripped off his clothes and beat him. Then they left him to die in the road.

A Jewish priest came down the road. But when he saw the dying man, he walked to the other side of the road. He did not help the man. Soon, another man came down the road. This man was a Levite, a helper of the priests. When he saw the dying man, he went and looked at him. Then, he walked on by. He did not help the man either.

Finally, a Samaritan came down the road. When he saw the dying man, he felt very sorry for him. He stopped and poured olive oil and wine on the man's wounds and then wrapped them in bandages. (Olive oil and wine were used as medicine; oil softened the wound and wine cleaned it.) Then the Samaritan gently placed the man on his own donkey and took him to an inn (motel). There, the Samaritan took care of the man. When the Samaritan had to leave, he gave some money to the innkeeper and said, "Take care of this man. If you spend more money on him than I have given you, I will pay you back when I come again."

When Jesus finished telling the story, he asked, "Which one of these three men was a neighbor to the man who was attacked by robbers?" The man who had asked, "Who is my neighbor?" answered, "The man who helped him." And Jesus said, "Then go and do the same thing he did!"

● ●

©1994 by Melissa C. Downey and Susan L. Lingo.
Permission is granted to reproduce this page for ministry use only—not for resale.

What did Jesus Mean?

There are many important meanings in Jesus' story of the good Samaritan. The first two men who saw the hurt man were religious men. One was a priest and the other one worked in the temple. Wouldn't you expect them to take care of the hurt man? The third man was a Samaritan—a person from Samaria. The Jewish people did not like people from Samaria. Jesus did not say for sure, but the man who was robbed and beaten up was probably Jewish, so he may have considered the Samaritan his enemy. Yet, the Samaritan stopped to help him and spent quite a bit of money on him.

What does this mean? Jesus was showing us that people who claim to be good do not always do good things. He was also showing us that we are to be kind to *everyone*—whether or not we like them or they like us! To "love your neighbor as you love yourself" is not always an easy thing to do. Do you like to be kind to someone who is mean to you? Is it easy to be kind to someone you don't know? The Samaritan didn't know the hurt man. But he helped him anyway.

In what ways was the Samaritan kind to the injured man? Unscramble the words below to find five ways the good Samaritan was kind. If you need help, look up Luke 10:34, 35.

_____   _____   _____
DANGABED   ISH   DNSOUW

____   ____   ____   ____   _____
TUP   IMH   NO   EHT   KEYNOD

_____   ____   ____   ____   ____
KOOT   IMH   OT   NA   NIN

_____   _____   ____   ____
TOKO   RACE   FO   IMH

_____   ____   _____
DIAP   HET   KINEENREP

©1994 by Melissa C. Downey and Susan L. Lingo.
Permission is granted to reproduce this page for ministry use only—not for resale.

Neighborly Way

Find your way thorough the maze by coloring the pictures of good neighbors.

©1994 by Melissa C. Downey and Susan L. Lingo.
Permission is granted to reproduce this page for ministry use only—not for resale.

Neighbors Are Nice

Will you be a good neighbor by helping to finish this poem? Select the rhyming words from the balloons to fill in the blanks.

A neighbor is someone
    you happen to _____,
At the playground, or store,
    or just down the _____.

He is someone who needs
    a friendly _____,
Or someone to play with him
    for a_____.

Someone who needs help
    when a pet can't be _____,
Or is new, and needs help
    in getting _____.

A neighbor is someone
    who may live next _____,"
Or may be someone
    you've not met _____.

Our neighbor is
    our fellow _____,
And we are to help him
    whenever we _____.

Kindness Code

What is the greatest kindness you can show to others? Decode the message to find out!

©1994 by Melissa C. Downey and Susan L. Lingo.
Permission is granted to reproduce this page for ministry use only—not for resale.

Matthew 19:19

Just how much should you care about your neighbor?
The children below are painting the memory verse on their
clubhouse. Can you help them? Color all the even numbers
red, all the odd numbers yellow.

©1994 by Melissa C. Downey and Susan L. Lingo.
Permission is granted to reproduce this page for ministry use only—not for resale.

A Good Neighbor Skit for Seven Characters:
Narrator, New Kid Nathan, Loud Larry, Tough Terry, Sweet Sally,
Friendly Frank, Kind Kris

Fill in the spaces with appropriate names to personalize the story.
Props needed: school books, notebooks, and papers

Scene 1

Narrator: If you were to tell the story of the Good Samaritan using things that
happen today, the story might sound something like this.
    A new kid named Nathan came to _____ school today. You
know, it's pretty rough being a new kid in school. Just look at Nathan.

(Nathan enters, looking a little panicked.)

Narrator: To him, this school must look huge!

(Loud Larry and Tough Terry enter, looking mean.)

Narrator: Oh no! Wouldn't you know it? The first kids to spot Nathan are the
big, bad bullies!

Loud Larry: Hey look! *(Shoves Terry to get his attention.)* There's a new kid!
Check him out!

Tough Terry: He doesn't look like much! Think we should show him the ropes?
(He laughs cruelly.)

Loud Larry: Naw, there goes the bell. We'll get him later.

Narrator: Whew! That was close! But knowing those two, they *will* get him
later!

Scene 2

(Nathan enters, carrying a bunch of books, walking slowly.)

Narrator: Nathan has made it through the day. The last bell has rung. The halls
are almost empty. Nathan is loaded with homework; look at the stack of
books he's carrying! *(Tough Terry and Loud Larry enter.)* Great! Here come the
big, bad guys!

©1994 by Melissa C. Downey and Susan L. Lingo.
Permission is granted to reproduce this page for ministry use only—not for resale.

Tough Terry: Hey! There's that new kid! Want to have some fun?

Loud Larry: Yeah! But we can't take too long—I've got to catch the bus.

Tough Terry: Hey, nerd! You gonna read all those books in one night? Here, let me help you out a little! *(Terry takes the top book from Nathan's stack and drops it on the floor.)*

Loud Larry: Hey, man, he needs more help than that! *(Larry knocks all the books out of Nathan's arms. Terry and Larry laugh as they kick books and scatter papers all over. They continue to laugh as they leave. Nathan stands still and looks sadly at his stuff all over the floor.)*

Narrator *(sadly):* Those two really know how to make a guy feel welcome. I wish someone would show Nathan that the kids at _____ school have some kindness. Here comes Sweet Sally. She's president of the fourth grade class. Friendly Frank is behind her. Surely they will help Nathan.

(Nathan is on his knees, slowly collecting papers and books.)

Sweet Sally *(walks right by):* Humph! What a nerd!

Friendly Frank *(walks over to Nathan, shaking his head):* Rough day, huh, dude? Better hurry or you'll miss the bus! *(Walks away.)*

Matthew *(enters and hurries over to Nathan):* Hey! Need some help?

Nathan *(looks up, not too sure about the offer. When Matthew smiles, Nathan returns the smile):* Yeah, I could use some help; I'm afraid I'll miss my bus.

Matthew: You're new here, aren't ya? Cool. I was new last year. *(Matthew finishes stacking the last of the books, stands up, and hands them to Nathan who has finished gathering the papers and also stood up.)* You must have Mrs. _____. She really piles on the homework, but she's OK.

Nathan: Thanks! Uh, I really need to catch the bus. I think it's number ____. Do you think it's gone yet?

Matthew: I hope not! That's my bus too! You're right; we'd better cruise! *(They begin walking quickly.)* You must not live too far from me. Hey! Some of the guys are coming over later—do you want to come over and meet them?

©1994 by Melissa C. Downey and Susan L. Lingo.
Permission is granted to reproduce this page for ministry use only—not for resale.

What Is Mercy?

Read the parable of the unmerciful (unforgiving) servant in your Bible. You will find it in Matthew 18:23-35.

To understand this parable, you must first understand what "mercy" is. Mercy is the quality of kindness and forgiveness. To be merciful to someone means to lovingly forgive them—even when they do not deserve forgiveness! A person's heart must be filled with loving kindness to be merciful. A person with a cold, hard heart is most likely to be unmerciful—like the servant in the story.

Jesus teaches about forgiveness in the parable of the unmerciful servant. The king was merciful to the servant when he told him that he did not have to pay what he owed. But instead of learning mercy from the king, the servant's heart was cold and hard when his friend asked for the same forgiveness. The servant did not forgive others as he had been forgiven! Because the servant showed no mercy, the king punished him.

A very important part of this story is the fact that the servant owed the king millions of dollars—so much that he could not pay the debt. When we do wrong things, say hurtful things, think ugly and hateful thoughts, we are sinning against others—and God. We can be sorry, but there is no way to "pay" for the things we have done—we owe what we cannot pay. Yet God, who is the King of Heaven and earth, is merciful to us; He sent Jesus to pay the price for our sins so that we can be forgiven.

"The Son paid for our sins, and in him we have forgiveness."

Colossians 1:14

The great lesson from this parable is that we must forgive others because we have been forgiven! Jesus has paid the debt that we owed. God, our King, has forgiven our sins. We do not want to be like the unmerciful servant who refused to forgive a little debt when he had been forgiven a BIG debt!

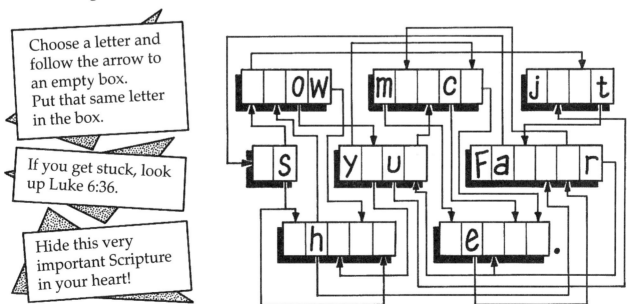

Choose a letter and follow the arrow to an empty box. Put that same letter in the box.

If you get stuck, look up Luke 6:36.

Hide this very important Scripture in your heart!

©1994 by Melissa C. Downey and Susan L. Lingo.
Permission is granted to reproduce this page for ministry use only—not for resale.

Mercy Me!

Unscramble the bold letters at the top of the first box to correctly spell another word for forgiveness. Write the bold letters in the correct order in the top of the empty box. Take the columns of words that appear under each bold letter in the first box and write them under the same letter in the empty box. When you are finished, read the words in the second box from left to right to see what will happen if you are like the unmerciful servant in Jesus' parable.

E	Y	M	R	C
if	men	"For	you	forgive
they	you,	when	sin	against
heavenly	also	your	Father	will
you.	you	forgive	But	if
not	their	do	forgive	men
your	not	sins,	Father	will
your		forgive	sins."	

©1994 by Melissa C. Downey and Susan L. Lingo.
Permission is granted to reproduce this page for ministry use only—not for resale.

Be kind and loving to each other.
Forgive each other just as
God forgave you in Christ.

Ephesians 4:32

To help you memorize this Scripture, color every part of the picture that contains a word from the verse. Be careful! There are some words that don't belong!

©1994 by Melissa C. Downey and Susan L. Lingo.
Permission is granted to reproduce this page for ministry use only—not for resale.

Jesus gave us gifts of wisdom in His wonderful parables. He taught us how to know God better and how to do the things that God wants us to do. Draw a picture of something that you've learned from the parables of Jesus.

©1994 by Melissa C. Downey and Susan L. Lingo.
Permission is granted to reproduce this page for ministry use only—not for resale.